KV-523-470

ALLEN PHOTOGRAPHIC GUIDES

TRAINING YOUR PUPPY

CONTENTS

INTRODUCTION

Your puppy is to be one of the family, a companion and a source of enjoyment. A responsive puppy helps to create a real partnership that will give great pleasure throughout his life. However, he can also be an embarrassment and cause great displeasure to yourself and others.

To make this lifetime partnership one of pleasure he requires understanding and basic training.

AN UNDERSTANDING

HOW DOES YOUR PUPPY LEARN?

Most of a puppy's learning is via the environment in which he lives, by the pleasant, or unpleasant, realities of day to day living. He will learn that by jumping up on you and others the social contact will give its own rewards. He also learns to pull on the lead because it gives him a sense of control, he has taken the Alpha status.

A responsive puppy helps to create a real partnership

Jumping up – a bad habit

Inducement not good enough to have the puppy's 'interest' coincide with that of the owner

Coming in for titbit without being asked to sit

'A puppy will always do what he considers to be in his best interest at that moment in time.' That quote will always determine the 'goods' and 'evils' of a puppy's approach to learning.

A puppy will learn from your actions – the meaning of any related verbal instruction will come later. If you want a puppy to sit you induce him to sit. This is done by movement, noise, physical contact, or a combination from all three. He is then rewarded.

He learns from actions that it is a pleasant experience to respond and, eventually, he learns the meaning of the words that go with the actions.

A puppy is taught by repeating an activity and from you rewarding him for a satisfactory response or the disappointment of your attitude to an unsatisfactory response. He learns through self-interest and self-preservation. How quickly he learns depends on his age, intelligence, the suitability of the training and the effect of that particular experience. A puppy's ability to concentrate is likely to be very limited but it develops with age and his enthusiasm to please.

THE ART OF COMMUNICATION

Your puppy must be able to understand your requirements before he can respond to them. This response is the basis for your future partnership.

To have your puppy react, his interest must be generated in the first instance, otherwise there is no link of communication between you and your puppy. That link must be secure before any form of contact can be meaningful.

Tap on croup for attention

To get a response when a puppy has such an interesting toy will require a strong 'interest generator'

An attentive puppy requires the correct approach to suit the situation

It is all about generating the puppy's interest, doing something with it, and rewarding him. This starts with his name – the most important interest generator. His name is probably the first word he understands. Initially, it is just a noise from your vocal cords. The sound is meaningless. It is a noise that attracts his attention but he will soon recognise this particular sound as his interest generator. To get a response your requirements must be suitably presented: a word, a phrase, a sentence, a clap of hands or a whistle. Any noise will achieve the desired result if used in the appropriate manner. You can also use body language, physically touch him, or make use of the appropriate equipment.

The intensity of your approach will be governed by the urgency of your requirements. There is no sense in hitting a puppy with a harsh voice if a gentle call of his name will generate his interest. It is also a waste of effort to use a soft and gentle approach if your puppy is too interested in some other activity.

Remember a prompt reaction to his name is the foundation to success. When you get his attention, use it and reward him. Puppies become creatures of habit and so long as the conditions are consistent their responses can also be expected to be consistent.

CONFLICT OF INTERESTS

Life with a puppy can easily become a conflict of interests; his interests against yours. Your ability to recognise a potential conflict is very important. When these interests merge there is agreement and harmony, but it can take time to achieve such a situation.

You should think before you act and create success rather than failure. It is not wise to exert authority beyond your measure of control. The distance between yourself and your puppy can affect his response. An untrained puppy which is insecure is likely to return on the call; but an independent pup with something else on his mind is likely to ignore such a call.

Puppy's response to the call to leave the slipper for his reward

REWARDS AND STOPPERS

Rewards and stoppers both play an important role. Rewards should always follow a puppy's activities which please you. You may wish to divert him from doing something innocent or otherwise and reward him for responding. Or you may wish to show your appreciation on completion of some request he has performed for you. This reward must always include praise, be it verbal, fondling, or both, but this can also include the use of food or play toys to create greater incentives for the future.

Reward of titbits for recall

Applying a stopper may be considered as part of the interest-generating approach but its application is usually by voice, short and sharp, and in a situation when urgency is being applied. It may be termed as unpleasant but its successful use should always be followed by your appreciation.

At times of great need a very forceful stopper may be used and can cause a puppy some stress. Such a stopper will only have a negative effect if the puppy is left in a confused or stressed state of mind. To counter this a sympathetic approach must be applied to allay any possible confusion or stress. Remember, puppies never misbehave. They only act in a manner that can displease you.

Various types of titbits

Rewards are training aids. In the form of titbits and toys they are complementary to praise. Such items can be used as inducements to achieve your purpose but, when used, these inducements must be given immediately on completion of your objective.

Some puppies respond to any type of titbit but the type that generates greatest interest is the most effective. Care must be given to prevent overfeeding with titbits, the smaller the better and many of the bought varieties can be broken up.

Titbit containers are very important. Dogs cannot see individual titbits at a distance therefore they should be kept in a plastic bag or a firm container that your puppy can see or hear when rattled.

Final presentation should induce your puppy to come in close to you. Hold the container along with a loose titbit in the clenched hand close to your body at the puppy's nose level. You may find it more convenient to be on your knees. As soon as the puppy sniffs at your hand, open it and let him take the titbit.

Play toys can also be used in training, particularly squeaky toys that help to engender excitement. However, the full benefit will result from the fun and games which follow as a reward.

Be it the giving of titbits or the throwing of toys, your own feelings of pleasure must be transmitted through to your puppy.

Titbits held too high encourages jumping up

How it should be done. Sitting nicely for a titbit

CONTROL EQUIPMENT

Controlling equipment has three principal purposes:

1. To give you the confidence to handle any situation and to convince your puppy it is in his best interest to co-operate.

2. To restrain your puppy when situations develop that are out of your control.

3. For control when it is inconvenient to give your puppy your full attention.

We are referring principally to collars and leads and the alternatives to these pieces of equipment.

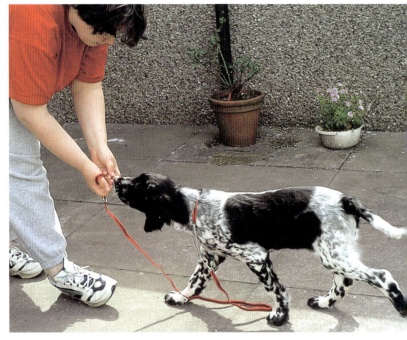

Induced recall on lead

With a Halti head harness

With a Lupi body harness

Check chain

COLLARS

There are many types of collar with each having some value, but the most suitable style is the Combi-collar. This collar has a short chain loop that helps to apply control with a minor checking action. There is also the Halti type of head harness and the Lupi style of body harness that can be useful for controlling unruly juniors. Both these harnesses are for juniors and older dogs that have missed out on proper initial training.

The collar is the most intimate piece of equipment your puppy will get to know and it is important that he is happy to have it fitted. In the name of safety, collars should be fitted with just sufficient 'slack' to be comfortable. A neat fit over the puppy's head is usually about right, although a much looser setting can be applied in training to accept fitting before the collar is left on for the day. The use of titbits will soon make this a pleasurable experience. It can also be a good policy to take the collar off each night and refit in the morning.

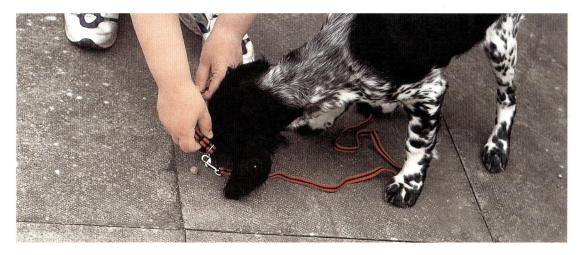

Titbit on ground to induce the head down to put the collar on

LEADS AND LINES

A quality lead you feel comfortable with will give you good service. The standard length of four to five feet (1.2 to 1.5 metres) serves both training and normal handling purposes. Chain leads are not recommended, they are hard on your hands.

Retractable or Flexi leads can be of value in training or for limited freedom when out exercising your puppy.

A thirty feet (9.2 metres) trailing line can have a useful inhibiting factor during training or normal exercising, especially with a piece of wood tied on the end. An over-boisterous junior will benefit from a six feet (1.8 metres) trailing line as an alternative. The short line also has indoor uses without the wood, loop or knots on the trailing end so that it cannot get caught under a door.

Ideally, these lines should be of lightweight nylon cord with a clip fixed on the end. The type of clip normally attached to a lead would suit.

Combi-collar and lead

Flexi-lead

Thirty feet long line to control at a distance

HOUSE TRAINING AND PROBLEM AVOIDANCE

Your puppy has just left his mother, his litter mates, the humans, the only home and smells he has known. He is under stress; he needs comfort and reassurance. If you can settle him into your home without problems you have made a good start.

Indoor kennel

There are a number of ways of getting a stressed puppy into a settled daily and nightly routine. A suitable bed is important, it may be a large cardboard box that will allow for the first few weeks of growth prior to a more permanent bed to accommodate his full growth. An indoor kennel can be considered as his own bit of space from day one. His bed must always be available and he should be encouraged to use it for resting.

A puppy's first few nights may be vital to his future conduct. Company for a few nights does help. I prefer to have a camp bed beside or near to him for three nights or so. It is good to be at hand to let him out if the need arises. Settling in with a comforter helps. A sterilised marrow bone with a smear of meat paste or spreading cheese can keep him occupied when left at night. This can be used at any time he is to be left on his own.

With a filled bone

HOUSE TRAINING

The rules of house training are simple, but understanding a puppy's needs is essential. Initially his needs are often and normally:

1. When he wakes up.

2. After feeding.

3. During or after excited play.

At odd times he will also be seen wandering round just thinking about it. If you miss the indications you are too late.

Puppies tend to use areas they have used before and a purposely placed paper for over-night use can restrict the puppy's intended target areas.

AVOIDING PROBLEMS

It is important that you should not be too demanding on your puppy but, if he understands your requirements, consider the effect of possible distractions before asking for an immediate response. If your action has not been effective, consider it to be your own misjudgement of the situation.

Always assess the situation where problems are likely to arise and think about the most likely route to success. Under similar circumstances, a puppy will always repeat a previous failure unless preventative action is taken.

Keeping a puppy out of trouble is not always easy but there are a few ideas that can help to generate interest for a little while without your full involvement.

A toy box with as many toys as you want but, like children, they always enjoy a new toy. During the time of teething, toys that are destructible can be useful. An empty washing up container (cleaned out) would do. A bought smoked or sterilised bone (never cooked) with spreading cheese or the like in the middle can occupy a little

An activity toy with food inside to keep a puppy amused can avoid many problems

mind. The same can be done with a Kong and an Activity Ball with pellets of dog food can have interesting results. To avoid him 'stealing' your items always introduce new toys by playing with him. When his scent is on it he will know it belongs to him.

The basic approach to training that follows will encourage a very co-operative attitude from your puppy and can be started at a very early age.

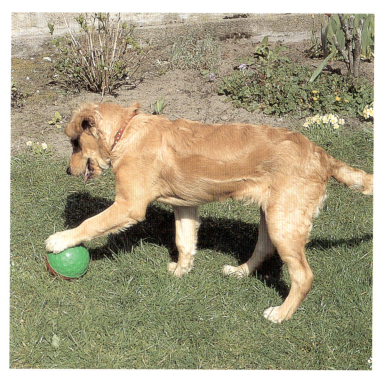

right Puzzled about how to get to the food

Finding food in an activity ball

A FOUNDATION FOR CONTROL

There are four components of control that are the foundation of a good relationship between you and your puppy.

1. To come back when called.

2. To walk on a loose lead.

3. To sit and stay.

4. To go down and stay.

As you will wish to prevent problems, the earlier and more informal your approach to the first two items the better. Starting with an older puppy which has bad habits will just take a bit longer.

You can begin by combining recall and lead training with the introductory stage of generating his interest.

GENERATING AND MAINTAINING INTEREST

An attentive puppy makes a good start

The objective is to obtain your puppy's interest in any situation and make use of it. Take advantage of his curiosity. Attract his attention by any means which work, but always include the use of his name. Rustle a bag, shake a box of titbits, squeak a toy or bounce a ball, but be excited as you call him. If he is within touching distance and doing his 'own thing', tap with your finger on his hindquarters as you call his name. As soon as you have his attention you have his interest, get him to come

Feeding bowl to induce recall

Investigating owner lying down

very close to you. Move backwards and draw him in if necessary, then reward and praise him. Build up a sense of **interest** and he will come in for a **reward**.

It is important that your voice changes to suit the situation. A little sharpness to get his attention then encouragement to maintain his interest. Use body language and include hands and arms. Just as one would welcome a small child, minimise the body stature by getting down to his level and this can promote his co-operation.

There are many natural situations which lend themselves to consolidation for a recall. When your puppy is coming towards you of his own accord, call him in gently, but with urgency. Every time you call, talk to him, '**Come** on son, in you **come**, that's a good boy'. Apply emphasis on the 'come'. Feeding time is an ideal occasion to make use of a recall.

Avoid calling for his attention when his interest is on something else, unless you are convinced that you can get him to respond. Avoid a conflict of interest you cannot handle. Assess the effect of distances and, if necessary, increase or decrease the distance between you and your puppy to achieve the desired effect. If you are to move towards him, do it quietly with unhurried movements. Never run after him, even in fun. As they grow older and faster they learn not to be caught.

If it is to be of any value, run away from him as you excitedly call him to follow. You can lie on the floor, hide your face and pretend to cry, this will often have the inquisitive mind of a puppy taking over and will bring him in. Praise, affection, titbits or toys, the choice is unimportant, if it works.

Learning to make use of the lead is now in order, with the objective of getting and keeping your puppy's interest for a short period. You now want him to respond to the call of his name and move towards you on a

How to hold the lead in the right hand

loose lead as you are moving backwards. You can change direction especially if his interest is being lost. Do anything exciting to keep that interest, but keep moving backwards for five to ten seconds. Finish by stopping when you have got him close to you. Immediately give a reward and excited praise.

Always start by using his name and, if he is distracted, immediately follow with a little tap on his hindquarters or a minor tug on the lead and a continuous flow of verbal encouragement, such as, **'come on son, hurry up… that's a good boy'.**

Your handling of the lead along with hand, arm and body actions are equally important. The loop at the end of the lead should be over the thumb of the right hand and, when necessary in the clenched hand.

When you are moving backwards your hands should, if possible, be kept at the puppy's eye level and the lead/collar attachment below the puppy's lower jaw. With the palms of the hands facing upwards, finger, arm and body movements are all used for encouragement. To create greater distance between you and your puppy a Flexi-lead can replace your lead.

Recall on Flexi-lead

COME BACK WHEN CALLED

By applying the routine to generate your puppy's interest the basis for calling your puppy back under more difficult circumstances is now in place. As puppies grow into young juveniles, the developing mind can create a streak of independence which will result in a conflict of interest from time to time. With the added distraction of the outside world, the conflicts become more apparent and must be overcome. The means already described can and should be continued and used at any time. However, they may require to be supplemented by a wider range of actions.

Short line. Do not use it to pull puppy in

Being encouraged to come in on a short line

The short or long line can now be utilised if necessary. The short trailing line can be used indoors or out. Indoors in particular, it can replace the lead and be left to trail behind the puppy, but for safety, only when in your company. You can stand on the end or pick it up to apply control.

Out of doors and, with the long trailing line, you can have some thirty feet (9.2 metres) between yourself and your puppy and still be in control. You can stand on the line to prevent him from moving away from you or you can pick it up. Never pull him in, use it as an extension of the lead.

Short line for indoor control

Becoming tangled on a long line can terminate excited activity

Short line with bar

No fun with a tangled line

Induce him to come to you with any or all means at your disposal, including backward movement. Draw the line in as he gets nearer. A very energetic puppy may run uncontrolled and care should be taken that nobody gets entangled with the line. His own entanglement is his problem and this can teach him to think before he gets into such a state in the future. The short line with a piece of wood tied on the end is an alternative. Again, his actions will cause his own discomfort and teach him to think first.

LOOSE LEAD WALKING

The described use of the lead for backward movement, especially where there is a distraction, is now the basis for walking on a loose lead. Changing from backward to forward movement is attained by moving to your puppy's right side so that he can turn in to your left side as you pass each other. Your left hand can move out to help guide the puppy into place at your left leg.

You are both walking in the same direction and lead control is important. The loop is still over your right thumb and the surplus lead can be gathered in the same hand.

Any attempt by the puppy to move ahead of you should be countered immediately by backward movement and the use of the left hand as necessary to retain his interest. He will soon learn to keep an eye on you and get to know his place.

Walking to heel

A rescue pup – changing from backward to forward movement

SIT AND STAY

There are two approaches to getting the puppy into a sit:

1. Sitting in front of you.

2. Sitting at your side.

The former can be carried out at any time. For example, on completion of your backward movement on the lead.

When your puppy is facing you, make use of titbits close to and at the puppy's nose height. Slowly draw your hands with the titbit up and close to your body with his head following; at the same time give verbal encouragement with the instruction 'sit'. As the head comes up the bottom goes down to sit, let him take the titbit, fondle his neck, turn and stand straddled over him to keep him sitting. Be prepared to prevent him from moving but use gentle and restrained praise.

Large-breed puppy sitting for titbit after backward movement

Small-breed puppy being trained to sit

Keeping a small puppy in sit position

Keeping a restless puppy in sit position; note thumbs in collar

Large breed kept in sit position with owner's hand caressing

Do not let him move until you are ready, but when you give him freedom from the sit be positive and let him know. For example, tell him 'O.K., son, up you get'.

When he knows how to sit in front on a verbal instruction, you can then use the same instruction to sit when he is by your left side.

You may need to give physical assistance. To do this, with puppy at your left side, take the lead at the collar in your right hand and use the left hand to apply pressure at his groin to put him into the sit. Again keep him there for a few seconds before you 'permit' him to get up.

left Helping the puppy to sit with left hand at the groin
right Being physically put into sit

DOWN AND STAY

Training to go down

An easy way to get your puppy down is to sit on the floor with a knee arched and tempt him down by drawing a titbit under the bent knee until he is down getting his reward. Again verbal encouragement with the instruction 'down' should be included. He can be kept down until you give him freedom.

Both 'sit' and 'down' to stay should be built up slowly in time and distance from your puppy.

Both you and your puppy will benefit from the mutual respect that develops through this form of basic training. As your puppy grows through adolescence into full maturity the training experiences you have both acquired will cement an enjoyable companionship which will last a life time.

Maintaining contact at down

Maintaining down

ACKNOWLEDGEMENTS

My thanks to Maureen Taylor of the Angus Canine Centre,
Monifieth, and Doreen Bidgood of the Rio Dog Training Classes,
Newport, Fife, for introducing me to a fine selection of puppies and
their owners: Hogan – Munsterlander; Ricky – Golden Retriever;
Harriet – St Bernard; Moss – Border Collie; Tui – Labrador;
Flora – Corgi and Ben – Cavalier King Charles Spaniel.

Dedication

To the First Scottish Branch (Dundee) of the Associated Sheep, Police
and Army Dog Society for introducing me to the art of dog training.

British Library Cataloguing-in-Publication Data.
A catalogue record for this book is available from the British Library

ISBN 0.85131.778.2

© John Cree 2000
John Cree asserts his right to be identified as the author of this work in
accordance with the Copyright, Design and Patent Act 1988

Published in Great Britain in 2000 by
J. A. Allen an imprint of Robert Hale Ltd.,
Clerkenwell House, 45–47 Clerkenwell Green,
London EC1R 0HT

Series design by Paul Saunders, layout by Terence Caven
Series editor John Beaton
Colour processing by Tenon & Polert Colour Scanning Ltd., Hong Kong
Printed in Hong Kong by Dah Hua International Printing Press Co. Ltd.